Gallery Books
Editor Peter Fallon

CARGO

Polina Cosgrave

CARGO

Gallery Books

Cargo
is first published
simultaneously in paperback
and in a clothbound edition
on 18 April 2024.

The Gallery Press
Loughcrew
Oldcastle
County Meath
Ireland

www.gallerypress.com

ISBN 978 1 91133 878 9 *paperback*
      978 1 91133 879 6 *clothbound*

A CIP catalogue record for this book
is available from the British Library.

Cargo receives financial assistance
from the Arts Council.

Contents

for Erika

Love, by its very nature, is unworldly, and it is for this reason rather than its rarity that it is not only apolitical but antipolitical, perhaps the most powerful of all antipolitical forces.

— Hannah Arendt

Apologies

My daughter, fists of fire, kiss of a panther.
If the sun had a voice it would be yours.
My daughter, steel bridges of lashes,
heart of a dinosaur, speed of an aircraft,

little body full of bees. The world you inherit:
we didn't mean it, we haven't known better.
Trust me, once upon a time there was freedom
of speech, freedom of travel, freedom of thought.

Before our straitjackets got too cosy you could
leave everything open: your door, your mind,
your future, even your ripe blackberries of eyes.
My daughter, with two languages arguing,
my daughter without measure,

my daughter, soul of the dawn,
my daughter, enemy of all order —
not everything locked is worth opening.
My daughter, my nightingale's song:
but this is not for them to decide
how you use your key.

Herbarium

Accept my apologies,
you shy chamomile of May.
I'm going to pluck you
and bestow your delicacy
upon my crying daughter.

You will be her joy this evening,
brought home in a little fist.
Reluctant to let go
of the newfound treasure
my little girl will take you to bed,
hold your stalk tight
even when looking for
my breast in the warm
semi-darkness of her room.

After she falls asleep
heavy with milk
her fist will unclench
revealing your crumpled crown.
Will I ever see anything as complete
and grounding as your fading
life on her pillow?

Accept my apologies,
you flawless man of May.
I'm going to pluck you
and bestow your splendour
upon my crying self.

You will be my joy this evening,
brought home . . .
Well, you get the idea.

Don't Make Love to Them If They Don't Dance

Don't make love to them if they don't dance,
if they don't drink, if they
do not treat their first breath
after waking up as a marvel.

If their feet can resist moving
to the devil's music,
if red wine doesn't fill
their belly with laughter,
do not take them in your bed.
It'd be colder with them in it.

Don't make friends with them if they don't cry,
if they don't read, if they
can't listen to a stranger
as if their life depends on it.
Chances are they stay deaf
to their own children.

If their mind can resist inhabiting
worlds full of magic,
if others' pain doesn't fill
their eyes with sorrow,
do not take them in your heart.
It'd be emptier with them in it.

Make peace with them.
Make for the exit.
Make something of yourself.
Make sure the sparks are flying high
from underneath your heels
when you're dancing like crazy
to the devil's music.

Mommy's Got a Gun

It's not us today.
Not your fussy kids,
not your ice-cold mother,
not your underpaid ex-wife, sounds turning into mercury
in her half-opened skull,
not your first teacher with his vampire heart and arthritic
    hands,
not your young lover, your bite —
a red half-moon on her soft botoxed lips.
All doomed. But not tonight.

Burning Man is not a festival anymore, not only a festival.
You saw Jah in your dreams growling 'I am',
a faith volcano erupted onto your stale bedsheets,
otherwise devoid of anything worth thinking of.
Not my type of god, you whispered,
before you almost pissed yourself.
Every day is a lake of fire we're swallowed by.
Every night is a bird missing from a welded cage.
Not tonight.

Because tonight you'll write till dawn
or punch the bag until your knuckles are blue
in the name of our species.
The rain has eight eyes like a spider
and we are being stalked by our future litter.
Open your textbooks, children, page 2023.
X is the capital of death.
X is the capital of nowhere.
Yet I sing your blood with each sign
in my Word Document.
Yet you will love me
like a missing limb that was about to kill.

Another Last One

I come to you
for one more joke,
one more smile,
one more touch.

It's going to be the last one,
I swear on my breast milk,
on the first edition of Dostoevsky,
on a glass of wine I'll drink after five dry years
and other things I hold sacred.

Little do you know
how I lie ablaze at 3 a.m.,
the mere thought of you
is a lit match,
and I burn alone in my bed.

I come for one more word.
A tiny dose of you should get me
through a couple of days.
I'm only having the one.

Little do you know
how I am secretly proud
of this human brain I possess
making me feel this way
about someone,

how I am carried forward
and out of the darkness
with a glaring thrust of life.

I come to you, a rocket.
I cannot
not kiss you anymore.

What Makes You Special

What makes you special
is how gently you hold
the beating heart of life
in the middle of your palm.
Thus you say:
I am here to teach and be taught,
to adore and be adored.
So are you, don't worry.

What makes you special
is how you open my mind
as a Christmas present.
With glitter blown off,
ribbon carefully cut,
I freeze unwrapped.
See me and understand:
I'm about to blow up
from this kind of intimacy.

I, so ordinary and plain,
abide by no rules,
carry no weapons.
Like a child
I encounter the world
in all its generosity.

And you —
a gust of autumn wind
over the lake,
a bite on my neck,
a chocolate bar
saved for after dinner.

I don't know what to do with you.

Cargo

Every night I hear planes
flying over our house
I count them like sheep
One, bringing death to a village
Two, bringing death to a city
Three, bringing food for the soldiers
who will finish the job
Four, bringing back the bodies

Every night I hear planes
flying over our house
They hum like a swarm of bees
One, making a U-turn
Two, heading back at high speed
Three, what if this one is coming after us
Four, aren't they all

Every night I hear planes
flying over our house
I asked around, no one else is bothered
Every night I hear planes
flying over our house
Not once did they wake up my child
smiling in her sleep

Every night I hear planes
Every day I hear planes
I shout over them
what I can't whisper into your ear

Elegy to Youth

We were the mighty wind of the steppe.
We were the wind caressing the fire, the river, the rock.
We flew through and above the abandoned factories,
the overgrown soccer fields, the crumbling railway stations,
the rusty bus stops. The packs of mad dogs would go silent
when we were passing by. We were the wind.

Sober on Monday mornings we hummed over the tenth
cup of coffee blacker than bruises on our young bodies,
'Today is summer, tomorrow is winter.'
We never waited for life to bring us to our knees —
always hit first, always kiss first. The naive wind.

We are the reprint of a letter long burned.
Remember me? I've never changed. Just blowing harder.
Remember our feet erased away by the midnight jig,
our minds soaked in tequila.
Even the stones in our kidneys were dancing.

We once opened the can of love and the reddish liquid
splattered all over the grassy plains,
all over our faces, and still
we can't wash it off. The steppe lingers on.

Rockets are Dreaming of You

Writers are dreaming of poems,
rockets are dreaming of space.
Chessboards are dreaming of pawns,
I haven't dreamt for days.

Lovers are dreaming of kisses.
Clowns are dreaming of tears.
Wake me from this, sweet Jesus,
I haven't dreamt for years.

Soldiers are dreaming of grenades.
Children are dreaming of flight.
I haven't dreamt for decades.
Wake me and lend me your light

so I can be like writers,
rockets, lovers and soldiers.
So I can watch my nightmares
blossoming over my shoulder:

these children were dreaming of grenades.
Those soldiers were dreaming of flight.
The country is cursed for decades
and no one can sleep at night.

Love Song for a Dream Boy

I've never been this naked. My soul
in a hammerlock.
I've never been this eager. All thoughts
underneath your pants.
Don't worry, they can't hear us.
Especially when we talk.
Don't bother, they won't see us.
Especially when we dance.

I know not what I'm doing. However
this taste is true.
I know not whom I'm doing. But duty
is not my god.
It feels like I've been blinded,
now all I can sense is you.
The skies are rife with thunder,
your touch is a lightning rod.

The Country of Nowhere

I feel the change,
and do you, do you, do you?
The skies are pulsing,
those buds begin to swell,
their green mouths shouting obscenities
into the flamboyant faces of insects.
The ground beneath us
already getting wet.

The craving is here.
So dark and thick
that it turns into pain,
the pain of not talking to you,
the pain of your fingers not stroking me,
your new jokes untold,
our joint laughter not electrifying
the air.

The pain is my twin sister
and I hold on to it, inhale it instead of your scent.
I clench at its empty palm
as if it were my last hope in the country of nowhere,
my escape hatch,
my fire exit.

In the name of this pain
I won't become a ghost.
I have already heard the door
of my own coffin closing.
I know there's life —
the proof of it is touch.

Our Will

Our will is everywhere, like rain. Our will
is to mix mud with blood.
Our will is the strange noise in someone else's lobby.
We are here to drown the living and burn the dead.
Nobody can help you.

Our will is turning children's dreams inside out.
It's our own will. Can't you see? We are not some slaves.
This will is ours only.
Our shrines, our fertile land, our women in our endless fields.
Every single thing belongs to us. Except ourselves.

We are busy lying silent in a cesspit
but the will speaks for us. Our national will.
Our heart is darkness, darkness thrice.
Our ship is a ghost one, our home is jail.

And why are you so surprised that our springtime
is wartime?
Our music, listen, sirens and bombardments!
Our will is everywhere, just like our leader's.

Maybe we'll outlive him. Or maybe you will.
Your neighbours bet on you while you're screaming in agony.
Come and see for yourself. He is well trained to scatter
the ashes from our nest dolls.

Bones of Thoughts

I need to know what makes
your juices bleed,
peel the messages underneath your messages,
eat steak from your broken plate,
bite hard on your glassy melon.
Because you'd let me.

Are you thinking about me in the modest sobriety of
    your gloom?
Do you choke on those bones of thoughts?
Do you dissolve into the false embrace of closed curtains?
What if I can prove your theorem in all the possible ways?
Does saying my name still summon your goosebumps?
How about my legs confessing fire to you?
How about my skin pledging allegiance to the flag of your
    skin?

Understand this:
I am melting each day
more and more,
joyfully and in vain.
Albeit, whenever I check,
there is always the same
amount of me left,
thrilled at the prospect
of running out.

A Force Like You

Where are those guillotine lips
to turn my face inside out,
those hands of perfect precision
to plant bombs in my crevices,
genius fingers to strike the crimson bells
in the begging chasm of me?

Where is that uncompromising tongue
to orchestrate the song of my breath
falling off the cliff of your shoulders?

Where is your voice
leading the last humanity out of me
and into the slaughter,
your gaze corroding the ballast of my ignorance?

Where is it now?
Your delicate silence
to locate my wandering shriek
and crush it like a fly in the fist?

Where is your heart
pushing the sunsets through my hips
to the starlit barbed wire of horizon,
hammering my breasts into purity,
rushing me into the river of wild laughter?

My mind is a tired carnivore
haunting you where you are absent,
chasing you when you stand still.
My ways are those of a berserk
fearing nothing but being himself.

I am a mirror full of other people,
a surface with ever-moving cracks;
objects in it are stranger than they appear.

So where the hell are you?

I have opened my door so wide
only a force like you can get in.

One Joke Away

Water your plants,
feed your golden fish,
listen to your sentimental CDs
while I'm selling my soul here
to see you once in the shower.

I would even flatter the prime minister
having swallowed the spit I was saving
for his perpetually blank face
if it could get me in there with you.
I'd chitchat with Stalin's corpse over coffee.
I'd suck on the decomposed mouth of Genghis Khan
(or perhaps his horse, if that's the price).
I'd salute American Super Heroes
if only it granted me the opportunity
to wrap you up in warm towels,
to hold your flushed cheeks in my hungering hands.

But dignity, but duty, but daily wash . . .
The stale bread of life crunches
like stones on our teeth.
Serpentine things get in the way
and between my light and your light,
blindsided, I fail to find that suite
where you lay tired from waiting for me;
leathery skin, open tap
and a bottle of whiskey half-drunk.

Hence, fractured me,
hence, another marriage,
hence, another cigarette,
another decade I keep looking,
keep delaying. Sure, come here,
I am, as are all, afraid.

Every time I try to touch God a little
I end up biting his hand until it bleeds.
The good news is: I'm one joke away
from trusting you with my uncertain heart.
Will you play that CD for me?

Room with Two Unknowns

Entering the room
where you sit
barefoot
leaning on
the back of the chair
arms crossed
shirt open

Entering the room
to tell you all of it
but my tongue
is a captured bird
ceiling fan stutters
in solidarity

Entering the kind of room
I swore I never would
in front of the registrar,
guests and witnesses

the room which you
a minute ago were certain
wouldn't fit us both
and yet

windows open, curtains shut,
the room with two unknowns,
your expression that of a local pickpocket
accidently getting his hands
on a Fabergé egg

Is it me entering the room
or the room me
with you in it

getting bigger and bigger
until the whole city can hear

a crack of the lock,
a flick of the switch,
a click of the lick?

Big Bottles, Big Rivers

I'm going to drink from big bottles
and swim in big rivers.
I'm going to honour the ruins
and talk to the graves.
I'm coming home, Mother,
will you make my bed?

I'll walk down the main street
wearing nothing but hope.
The boy who left me will stare at me in horror.
He has always had the talent
to recognize a ghost among the living.
The boy I left will turn away in disgust.
I have aged painfully, and he is still nineteen
and seeing me at the bottom of every bottle,
burying me on the bottom of every river.

I'll sit with the memory
in the old pub.
I'll write letters to an Irishman
on the napkins
lined like
his mesmerizing hands.
I'll gulp down the need for him
settled as a lump in my throat
for it only to return
the morning after
twice as strong.

I will wake up in the bed
my mother made for me
wishing he could finish my bottle
and jump into my river.

Pine Cones, Sticks and Stones

Half-awake, I have mistaken
the pale sunrise outside the window
for Russian winter.
It seems the world turned
white and crisp behind the curtain.
Just like that time
when storm Emma hit Ireland
I took the last bus to your house
and we were trapped together for days.

We built a snowman larger than the two of us
in a shimmering field that had neither beginning
nor end, the same one you played in as a boy.
Ever since the storm passed
I'd go searching for the snowman's remains —
pine cones, sticks and stones,
but the field would not reveal them for me.

How do you bring a melted snowman back to life?
Until I know that
I will get my eyes drunk
on the milk of morning light.

Slavic Bride

Recognize me, you youngest son.
You troublemaker, you pain in the neck.
I am the wolf that ate your royal horse,
then showed you where
the magic firebird lives,
but clearly it wasn't enough
to make amends.

You are so impatient to touch forbidden things.
I saved you from certain death time and time again.
I carried you, your pride, your wrath, your women,
on my dishonoured back.

Oh, I am a wolf of many talents.
You ride me like a mare,
kiss me as if I am a virgin.
You ask me riddles, so I have become a sage.

Beware, the time has come — I owe you no more.
The skeleton of your horse has long turned to ashes.
Proceed alone with your kingly quests.

And if I ever find your breathless body,
tormented by the vultures, thirsty for
my water of death,
my water of life,
I'll deal with you as Code of Wolves requires.
From decay and back to me you shall rise
exuberant like a little pup.

Two Worlds

Deserted town
outside my door —
a quiet afternoon.
Phantom whispers
in the playground,
sun shining for no one but me.
A frozen bag of dog shit
but no dogs
outside my door.
They only howl at night;
that's how I know they live around.
No toddlers on the rusty swings,
no teenage girls
smoking in the lane,
animating Fernhill
with their sparrow chirping.
No seagulls arguing
outside my door
looking for some treats,
always ready to take off.
Light is eating my eyes out
with the big spoon of its omnipresence
outside my door.
Wind sucking on my breath.
In another world
people are marching
shoulder to shoulder in a pandemic.
I recognize some of the protesters:
I was married to that man
and all these furrows on his forehead are new;
that woman's lips used to move in such a way
I almost believed she loved me back.
Her features distorted now.
I watch thousands being synchronized,
they keep up with each other's grief.

The air full of scams
outside their doors.
This weather
turns their faces inside out or maybe
the batons of police do.
They march because there is no peace
outside their doors,
inside their doors.
Detuned music of the future
calls them to the streets
to break the bones of yesterday.
For everything is stolen
including
their doors.
So, they go out to kiss each other
and play soccer
with policemen's helmets.
Meanwhile
my life is lying on the crossroads
with its skirt hiked up.

Non-alcoholic

In the evenings
I have no other drink
than the air between the pines.
My routine is that
of a stone's mossy side,
of algae hugging the pebble.
Oh light, let me go.
I'm all whispers and no words.
Shall we sell this sunset
to someone better,
more pristine and jewel-like?

In my fishnets I glide
down the waterfalls of rage,
across the meadows of disgust
and into a taxi's maw.
Drive, drive along the muddy stream
with an expression hard as a rock in a throat
but don't be fooled by my awkward step.
My knuckles are one solid scream of brass,
the rapiers of my heels are what
pierced all those holes in your moon.
I've only had the air between the pines today,
and I seep through the ground
because I really want to.
Oh light, follow me,
will you?

Princess

I haven't seen your mother since.
The girls you used to scare the shit out of
got themselves cheap cars
and even cheaper husbands.

The black tomcat you fed your dinners to
turned out to be pregnant.
Her only kitten born dead is buried
next to the fir tree
we drank under
while skipping classes.

The jail you were hell-bent
on working in
is painted blue now.
The writing on your bedroom wall
'I am a woman. Thus, I am an actress'
was painted over.

In my dreams you said
you've been travelling the world
for fifteen years.
All these funky stories —
you surfing in Mozambique,
selling gold in Dubai,
driving trucks in Alaska —
I promised to pass on to your mother.

Just as you once swore
to call me the next morning
standing knee-deep
in the last year's snow.
Just as ever after
I swear to love them hard
before they go.

The Knocking

Our song pours and pours
into the lilac light,
onto the auburn ground,
pulled out of the gloom of our rooms
by the tinkling strings of tomorrow.

I dreamt I had you in my arms,
head pressed against my collarbone,
against the creeping morning,
against the whole goddamned humanity.

Our song has crawled
from underneath our beds
and into the city,
marked every roof,
ruffled every dove's feathers.

Our song is here, it has found us.
Knock-knock on your door right now,
claiming it will be merciful
if you open up.

Admit the finality of it:
can't stop that imminent climax,
that militant rhythm.
Pass me my gun,
my psalter and my love for you.
We shall follow that melody
wherever it leads.

Vortex

This region is now 'hosting' refugees.
Mostly children.
Embraced by your messages,
protected by the walls I grew up in,
I fall asleep. The roof is falling apart,
just like this country's present.
You protect the heart of me.

I only call you by your name,
common to your people,
to my ear — a rare bird trill.
Never 'baby'.
I talk to you with my life.
You always know how to respond.

Catapulted into the steppe,
this longing separates
me from my physical body.
Rusty buses. Separating
families from their land.
Retina collapses under the weight
of khaki colour, can't hold back
the water of me.

Hand on a mobile device,
I take an oath
to love you in any language.
Will you forgive me
in your native one?

Irish Sahara

You left it bone-dry,
left it craving for the rain
of your promises, for a glass
of care half-full.

Now you come back to the desert
of our lives asking us
to drink from your lips.

Sorry. Nobody here
to experience thirst. Each drop

evaporates.
Each human erased.

Splinter

Your image went through me
like a yellow Ferrari
passing a beggar under the bridge.

I swear you were here,
a golden meteor
at the speed of sound.
Gone in one blink.

Your godlike motion
left a dazzling splinter
of light in my retina.

Dare look
into my poisoned eyes
oozing love.

Them Too

Spread you
like butter on my bread,
like the wings of a hawk in my sky,
like a rainbow over the Northside.
Savour your colours,
as if they were the facets of a disco ball
I'm dancing under.

Spread you
like a magical ointment
all over the aching joints of my life.
Inhale the very vapour of you,
as if you were the love of my lungs.

Spread the news of you
to shake the drowsy world
that went numb
with too much anaesthesia,
too little heart.
Glorify your power,
as if you were the king of my secret lands,
the prophet of my body.

Spread them too,
in front of your alabaster torso,
two lily petals rising and bending
to demonstrate the sticky stigma,
as if it is the last one you'll own.

When We Shared the Bed

When we finally shared the bed
the Moon and the Stars came to watch us
weaving our hands and feet together.

Noticing how softly
you pinned me to the mattress
the Moon said:
'I will embellish their human fabric
with a silver thread of my own shine.'

And a drop of light slid in between,
our skins stretched out
on the moving blue covers.

Marvelling at how tirelessly
you were stitching me to the sheets
the Stars had spoken too:
'We wish to spill some pearly beads
upon the pattern so sublime.'

And everywhere we touched
a liquid glimmer showed up.

A single-hearted master,
you toiled away
until I fit you like a glove,
until celestial bodies
and bodies terrestrial
were the same
in our eyes.

As you were drifting off to sleep
like an infant on my chest,
after all your hard and fancy work,

I understood that I had been embroidered on you
all along
and could be seen from high above.

Second Coming

Where the Blues defy time,
where marble breasts define rhyme,
when a spark re-enters your body,
I will be ready lying on
my stomach still smouldering
with lungs alert
to your breath above,
with shoulder blades
aching with ecstasy,
just put your palm
between them
and you'll know.

Username

The practice of labelling
new occurrences
still relevant in the second half of life
is a bliss, a rarity.
A delusion.

But something unites
a lover's phone calls left unanswered
on a long balmy night,
a heartbeat suddenly dying down
on a faulty monitor,
a mob quietened by a story too real,
walking out of the cinema hall
with their glances turned inward.

More subtle than a change
between the daybreak
in July and August,
as urgent as a suicide note of an addict,

and if a name must be given here
it's going to be one of yours.

Eyeful

My fingers warmer now
in the pockets of your coat.
The wind has brought a shade
of cerise to your cheeks. I know it,
but dare not look.

I would put this evening
where I've always kept
the most important items.
My baby's hospital tag.
My town's commemorative coin.
My friend's last photograph.

The place I should clear out
for things of beauty to settle in.
It can't contain more than
an eyeful of you.

I steal one of your breaths
and my chest breaks open.
November sunbeams
burnt onto sternum.

Wings

That smooth loss of gravity
after the plane takes off,
moving the clouds apart
with its shiny head,
that perfect sinking feeling
always expected, yet always sudden,
time is almost brought to a halt,
light slowly touching faces
through a weeping porthole,
then a determined thrust
and a gentle release,
weightlessness achieved,
tasted by every muscle,
the whole body jolts
begging to be dropped again
with care.

Usually Empty

After you haven't talked with anyone for days,
your tongue shrivelled like a daffodil
nobody ever sees,
your speech
a cheap shiny trinket,
an unnecessary accessory
to that thing you are, i.e. a habit of breathing,
and you crawl along the seashore
just as your reptile brain suggested,
with your child attached to you
like a lifebuoy,
and see this guy with two guitars
sitting on the crooked bench
which is *usually empty*
and he looks you in the eye
as if you actually existed,
you smile at him,
and before you both know it
you are singing
The Cranberries' song,
and then another one,
because you mention
that you found a pirate copy
of their album back in Russia
when you were nine,
which blew your mind
and taught you some English,
now he says you've a great voice,
and your child looks at you
in utter disapproval,
because she hasn't learned to express
in any other way
just how much she thinks you suck at performing,
then it starts to rain furiously,
and he reveals that the other guitar

that he has been minding
belongs to the bloke
who lives under the bridge,
you both know him,
the Lithuanian one,
the owner of that beautiful dog
with black ears,
he likes to dye her side pink,
and he has a savage name,
and he possesses this guitar,
and now you're on the track
to bring it back to him,
and the three of you keep looking
for Ugo
near the river,
at the bus stops,
in the park,
the rain insists on being
effortless
and you suddenly
feel connected
you remember
that's why
you stayed in Ireland,
no, that's why
you stayed alive.

Dancing in Times of Fratricide

Civilian casualties. A common denominator.
Shock waves reach our minds.
Maternal instinct hurts the body
when nursery schools are bombed.

Girls fall in the changing room,
all quiet now, unhinged.
Paper dolls with loose limbs.
One says:
'I feel as if it's happening to me.'
Others sob and nod.
Some admit not sleeping for days.
'If you squat for one hour straight
the anxiety will vanish.'
After the class
each dancer is waiting
till the rest are dressed and ready to go.
'No air-raid shelter in this building.'
Seven of us
in a tiny jar of elevator,
empty corridors,
nobody left behind.
Six of us
returning home to their men.

Whoever you touch you always touch me.
Whenever one of them dies it is you.

Negative Space

You are what you've chosen to live without.
Your breath fills the space between the petals
of an orchid, exchanged for its aroma.
Smell it again to remember this day.
You are what you've chosen to repeat.

I repeat your name to warm my throat.
You grow like silence in full dark.
I repeat your face to tame the mayhem in my head.
It blooms all night long.
I repeat your gaze falling on my body,
gripping it like a net of promises.
I repeat your taste in my lonely mouth,
your lips on my fingers,
I repeat it until my mind is spent
and I'm all you
without you.

Let's Snow

Let's talk about this milky weather.
Let's talk all things melting away
and that one thing faithful.
Things cautiously planned and the one
out of our hands.
I've a snowflake in my mouth.
I stick my tongue out, and it creams into the night.

Let's talk about this winter,
how her wrinkled dress glows.
Let's talk about what became
of my mind's frozen chambers
at once lit up by the torch
of your understanding.

How you moulded me
into a moving sculpture
without wearing a glove.
About your will reversing me
the way they dreamt to reverse
Northern rivers. I hold
and hold onto the boring borders,
only for you to spill me out again.

Let's talk about my snowflake. Let's not.
Mulled wine makes me laugh just like you,
makes the snowflake dance faster.
Let's snow and swirl.
Then drink the thaw.

This Is My Desire

I want to shave my skull and peel off my skin,
wash this body away. Because my hunger is
awakening. Life is awakening within me.
I want to take off my face and burn all
that is hidden behind it. Dissect my narratives,
destroy the language that feeds on my meat,
destroy the meat that creates
this language. It bears no resemblance to me.
I have better things to remember

like the taste of my mother's milk,
like the breath of my first lover,
like the sunrise after my acid trip,
and how she kissed my open mouth,
and how she kissed my open mouth,
and how she kissed my open mouth.

I want to write my name all over her body
3500 times with my languageless tongue
to turn it into an unreadable symbol,
to turn her into a manuscript of fire.

I saw you in my dreams. Your hair got red.

Of Pears and Dragons

Lightbulbs in our garden,
decorative glassy fruits.
One shattered, two cracked.
Next to the overripe
November pears hanging low.
Some on the ground. With chunks
of gritty flesh bitten out
by unknown soaring guests.

A dragon must have eaten them,
I explain to my daughter.
But first he had broken our lightbulbs
so we couldn't notice him, so you wouldn't get scared.
The dragon we welcome in our home,
and never see: the Halloween fireworks,
his job too. He is always hiding
to keep us safe, I tell her.

However, he somewhat cares,
as dragons can, cold-blooded,
fear-mongering. So he leaves
a few signs of his presence.
And when my daughter is asleep
I come out into our garden
to have a chat with my pet dragon
about his glorious days, his frequent

flights, and all the fatherless children
he gets to entertain.

Every Second

I know every second of you,
my eyesight forever tied to your little fingers.
You ask with a sonorous giggle
and, yes, I would lay the world at your feet;
let's start with this plush dinosaur.
The happiness you have brought
into the catacombs of my life
is often more than I can take. But I am learning.

Every second of you is a lightning bolt
and a diamond falling into my lap.
What am I going to do with all this magnificence?
Me, a beggar, a stranger, a fraud?
I have stolen from Time itself.
Now I can see its hollow face
surveying me watching you bloom.
It has a Mona Lisa's smile
and fifteen rows of megalodon teeth.

A friend asks what it's like to have kids.
It's a knife at your throat
for the rest of your life.

Saturation

I ask the air to talk to me.
I plead.
The air is war.
A shrapnel wound. I bleed.
This blood is promising.
A word in every drop.
I want your chromosome.
I do. I don't.
Don't stop.

Francis

The morning after I'm tracing
the route of your tongue.
Invisible tattoos left
all over my thighs,
exactly as I imagined.

Your kisses only come off
with the face I'm wearing,
skin sealed like an envelope
by the same mouth
in myriads of ways.

My space hurts with the absence
of your breath, but that
is the perfect pain of being.
Walls blank and cold
without our shadows dancing.

I peel layer after layer of self
to get where you've never been
and invite you back in.

I am your room, here to contain it all.

Future Faking

On an average morning, just like this one,
yes, a boring morning in mid-October
(or pick a more suitable month, my love),
when the sleep-deprived parents will
be sorting their jolly (and not-so-jolly)
offspring into the local crèches and playschools,
and the snake of traffic will start
to dance and wriggle and the bakeries
will exude the smell of life so plentiful,
one of the children will definitely start
crying next to the entrance, and one
of the breads will certainly get burned,
and one of the cars will break down,

we'll hear a clap and see smoke
and immediately we'll feel
that the autocrat is dead. Don't ask me
how, but we'll know. His unnatural
reign will have lasted for so many
shameful decades. Despite our hatred
we will have been carrying his presence
in our exhausted minds through rain,
snow, financial and moral ruin,
like chronic illness. Now exhale
and watch that heavy ball of black light
leave your body. The air tastes different.
Cry along with the child at the playschool

entrance, call the mechanic to fix the engine,
and take a bite of that burned baguette:
nothing will ever taste this good again.

Amalgamation

Swans flying over the pond:
the sound of their wings stays.

Water changes colour
when our figures merge into one.

Your eyes change colour
every time I blink.

I ask April
to burn hotter,
so we both feel at home.

Our lips melt away with the words
stuck on them,
now we are also

over this pond:
white shadows of beauty
instead of beauty itself.

Fisherman's Perspective

He caught her like a trout
on a glistening hook of his penis
and reeled her in.
The timing was impeccable.
A sickening jolt pulled her out of the sea
and she still sees herself flying

over the emerald waves and the dancing boats,
the harbour sinking in coral and pink
reflected from the cirrus clouds,
over little burgundy roofs,
the flea market, the butcher's shop,
the old church spire,
the derelict building of her secondary school,
the pub they first held hands in,
over the unconcerned village,
and higher into the atmosphere,
until her mind is hollowed,
her blood is clear.

From where he stood, proud and grinning,
he could almost hear a faint whisper:
release me, baby.
I'm suffocating.

Grammar Drills

I wear your sentences
around my waist
like a leather garter belt,
with pride and pleasure.

Most precious phrases
have travelled
to my solar plexus.
I send them along
the blood flow
when no one's watching
and take joy in probing
wherever they settle down.

Red marks rooted in my body
are your way of teaching me
how it's done.
I carry them every hour of the day:
the promise of your shoulders
nesting under the daring weight of my legs,

your hips widening my world view,
and your native tongue,
a vibrating strip
of darkest beauty,
a jet of boiling truth
searching for a new meaning

between my thighs,

unsealing bated breath.
I'm learning this grammar by heart:
keep giving everything I have
until there's nothing left
of you, stranger.

Method

The man I love
is not like you.
He rides hell horses
and shoots big guns.
Fate is his bullet,
diamonds in his whiskey.
All the ladies know his name.

The man I love
could carve your heart out
with his playful knife
if I asked him to.
Instead he peels
an apple for me.
I eat a sour slice
right off the blade.

This man, just look
how smooth his gait is
when he carries me out
of the burning building
I used to call home.
Kindness is his opium.

The man I love
is not like you.
He puts his fingers
in my bloody mouth
and gets out the truth.

Acknowledgements

Acknowledgements are due to the editors of the following publications where some of these poems, or versions of them, were published or broadcast first: *Abridged, Apricot Press, Crannóg, Drawn to the Light Press, EastWest Literary Forum, Free the Verse, The Poetry Programme* (RTÉ Radio One), *Smashing Times* and *Studi irlandesi* (Firenze University Press).